What People Say About
Rhoberta Shaler, PhD . . .

You always impress me with your words of wisdom!!!
- Nadia S., Edmonton, AB

I really enjoyed your writing today. It not only simplified things,
it gave me hope. - Tom

Thank you for enriching my professional and day-by-day life. Receiving
and reading your [articles] has become a very enjoyable activity.
I appreciate the human way you write and describe your different
experiences. I would say that is a rare quality these days.
- Marcus P., Italy

I want to take a few moments to let you know how much I enjoy your
daily inspiration. Your thoughts have definitely kept my attitude positive
and have challenged me to reach deeper within myself and also to
reach further beyond my grasp.
- Leanna

You share parts of your life and yourself with those of
us who read this . . . I think that is much more important than anything
else you can do. Thank you for the impact you make on my life.
- Darlene G., TX

May I take this opportunity to tell you, your advice has had a great
impact on my life and I am now living a healthier and happier life
thanks to your articles. - Mangla S., UK

Other Books by Rhoberta Shaler, PhD

Optimize Your Day: Practical Wisdom for Optimal Living
What You Pay Attention To Expands. Focus Your Thinking.
   Change Your Results.
Wrestling Rhinos: Conquering Conflict in the Wilds of Work

Keep *it in* MIND

Memorable
Messages
for Staying
On Track

Rhoberta Shaler, PhD

www.OptimizeInstitute.com

Rhoberta Shaler, PhD
KEEP IT IN MIND! Memorable Messages for Staying On Track
ISBN: 0-9711689-1-1

Cover design and book layout by
somethingelse web+graphics, www.time4somethingelse.com

Cover photo of Dr. Shaler © 2004 Joanna Herr,
Herr Photography, Encinitas, CA
Additional cover photos courtesy of www.istockphoto.com

Published by People Skills Press, San Diego CA

For information, contact:
Rhoberta Shaler, PhD
Optimize! Institute™, San Diego CA
Email: info@OptimizeInstitute.com
Website: www.OptimizeInstitute.com

Contents

A different world cannot be created by indifferent people.

Unknown

Introduction

Thirty-six years ago, a book came into my life that changed my mind. In fact, after reading it, it was impossible to be the same as I had been before it dropped off the shelf. It rocked my thinking and awakened my understanding of personal responsibility. The fresh view it gave me of what was possible changed my perception of myself. I have always been grateful. What an amazing gift that was to a twenty-year old!

That book was *Psycho-Cybernetics* by Maxwell Maltz. It was one of the first popular books that talked about how to get more living out of life, how to transform life through choice. That was the beginning. The journey has continued–learning, reading, thinking, integrating, implementing, experimenting. As a therapist, I have walked this same path with many, many clients. Some were quite unwilling to embrace the all-important concept of self-responsibility. Why? Because they were equally unwilling to accept the need to demonstrate self-respect. It was easier to look for someone to blame for their lives than to change their self-image. Fortunately, most came to see themselves differently. As they did, they realized the power of their thoughts and choices. They changed the ways in which they saw themselves. Going from powerless to powerful, from reactive to responsive, makes all the difference.

I wrote this book to offer you some insights and ideas that can quickly change your life for the better. When I asked my daughter, my oldest child, what the most important lesson she felt I had taught her was, she wrote, "That I am 100% responsible and accountable for creating my own life the way I want it. If I wait for someone or something else to provide it, I'll be waiting a very long time."

That's my girl! Knowing that has made all the difference in my life. And, that is the message I offer to you. You are powerful. You are making choices hundreds of times each day. Choose wisely and create success on your own terms.

Keep it in mind.

I wish you well,

Rhoberta Shaler
Optimize Life Now!
San Diego, CA

January, 2003.

People take different roads seeking fulfillment and happiness. Just because they're not on your road doesn't mean they've gotten lost.

H. Jackson Brown, Jr.

F our little words sum up what has lifted most successful individuals above the crowed: a little bit more. They did all that was expected of them and a little bit more.

A. Lou Vickery

Are You a Success Type?

Do you have a "success-type" personality? Here are the ingredients: a sense of direction, understanding, courage, charity, self-esteem, self-confidence and self-acceptance.

The interesting thing about a sense of direction is that it needs to be maintained. Some folks think that when they achieve something, they have arrived. The truth is that arrival platform is the next departure platform and you do not want to spend much time in the station! You know that a bicycle only maintains its poise and equilibrium when it is moving forward. Bicycles do not maintain balance well while you are attempting to sit still, do they? Neither do lives.

Understanding depends upon good communication. In order to react appropriately you must listen well. This means setting aside your own interpretations and opinions sometimes and observing "Just the facts, Ma'am." Look for and seek out true information concerning yourself, your challenges, other people, their feelings and situations. Admit any mistakes you may have made, correct them and move forward.

Courage translates goals, desires and beliefs into realities. Nothing in this world comes with a guarantee. Often the difference between a successful person and a failure is not one's better abilities nor ideas, but the courage that one has to bet on the ideas, to take a calculated risk–and to act.

Successful people have some interest in and regard for other people. They respect others' issues and needs and recognize that every person deserves dignity and respect. Develop a genuine appreciation for other folks. Take the time to understand their feelings, viewpoints, desires and needs. Treat folks in ways that let them know that they are important.

Low self-esteem is a vice. It is an indulgence, really. A person with adequate self-esteem does not feel hostile toward others, isn't out to prove anything, sees facts clearly and is not demanding in his or her claims on other people. One quick way to improve your self-esteem is to appreciate and respect other folks more. When you treat other people as though they have value, your self-esteem will also improve.

Build your self-confidence by focusing on your past successes. You've had many. Focus on the learning you have gleaned from your life so far. Call up the feelings you have experienced when you have been successful and remember them. Relive your brave moments and you will be surprised at the increase in your courage.

You must have a degree of self-acceptance to be successful and happy. Most of us are better, wiser, stronger, more competent right now that we realize! Creating a better self-image does not create new abilities, talents, powers–it releases and utilizes them. Accept yourself as you are.

Build your own "success-type" personality!

Keep it in mind!

There are no traffic jams when you go the extra mile.

Anonymous

Trust each other again and again. When the trust level gets high enough, people transcend apparent limits, discovering new and awesome abilities for which they were previously unaware.

David Armistead

Be Responsible

How do you approach the people and situations in your life? Do you expect each person you meet to be trustworthy? Do you expect a positive outcome from each situation? Do you accord yourself love, respect and approval for who you are right this minute? Deciding to live from a place of acceptance and expectation of good seems to me to be "throwing your heart out in front of you". If you expect to get hurt, it is likely it will be so. If you expect to fail, that, too, is likely. Why? Because you give everything the meaning that it has for you. You project your expectations and create the behavior to play them out. You are that powerful.

There is no escaping the fact that you choose your attitudes and perceptions, your responses and behaviors. Your world would change miraculously if you took full responsibility for your own life. Imagine a world without blame, a world of empowered people, genuinely interested in one another, responsible and accountable!

From today on, be one of those people. Take responsibility for your actions, perceptions, feelings and projections. Say so. Affirm it. "I take responsibility for everything I think, say, feel and do." Then, throw your heart out in front of you and run ahead to catch it!

Keep it in mind!

A successful individual typically sets his next goal somewhat but not too much above his last achievement. In this way he steadily raises his level of aspiration.

Kurt Lewin

Day-Tight Compartments

In his book, *A Way of Life*, William Osler suggested it was wise to live life in "day-tight compartments". He felt it was important to look neither forward nor backward beyond a twenty-four hour cycle. It was important, he said, to live each day in the best way possible because you would then be doing the most within your power to make tomorrow better. Osler was suggesting the same thing that Alcoholics Anonymous advocate: Don't try to stop drinking forever but "Just for Today". Are you focusing on "do-able" chunks or on goals so large that they seem daunting?

Break your largest goals into manageable pieces. You probably know the story of the woman who approached the famous concert pianist following a breathtaking recital and said to him, "I would give my life to be able to play like that!" And he said, "Madam, I did." And he did it one day at a time, one scale at a time, one phrase at a time. Any task, skill or goal can be reached when you are ready, willing and able to take the right steps in the right order. The wisdom lies in creating the map, doesn't it?

Once you have the map, stay on the path. You've done the "big picture thinking." Now, focus on your next step. Move forward remembering Lao-Tzu's' words: "The journey of a thousand miles begins with one step."

Keep it in mind!

Often we allow ourselves to be upset by small things we should despise and forget. We lose many irreplaceable hours brooding over grievances that, in a year's time, will be for-gotten by us and by everybody. No, let us devote our life to worthwhile actions and feelings, to great thoughts, real affections and enduring undertakings.

Andre Maurois

Mountain Climbing Over Molehills

Someone has said that the greatest cause of ulcers is mountain-climbing over mole-hills! Is that the way you get your exercise?

Many folks allow themselves to be thrown off course by minor or imaginary threats. Often they interpret these as life-or-death, or do-or-die situations. They put so much energy into their worries that there is none available for progress. Some even believe that worrying demonstrates caring. This is misguided, too.

The use you make of your energy is your choice. Simply use it consciously and constructively. Worry is neither.

Bertrand Russell, philosopher and mathematician, tells of a technique he used on himself to calm down his worries and excessive negative excitement:

> *"When some misfortune threatens, consider seriously and deliberately what is the very worst that could possibly happen. Having looked this possible misfortune in the face, give yourself sound reasons for thinking that after all it would be no such very terrible disaster. Such reasons always exist, since at the worst, nothing that happens to oneself has any cosmic importance. When you have looked for some time steadily at the worst possibility and have said to yourself with real conviction, 'Well, after all, that would not matter so very much,' you will find that your worry diminishes to a quite extraordinary extent. It may be necessary to repeat the process*

*a few times, but in the end, if you have shirked nothing
in facing the worse possible issue, you will find that your
worry disappears altogether and is replaced by a kind of
exhilaration.*"

Now that seems worth having, doesn't it? Exhilaration brings
energy to push through difficulties and level mountains as well as
mole-hills.

This strategy for approaching your concerns can help you
to maintain an assertive, goal-directed, self-determining attitude
even in the presence of very real and serious threats and dangers.
Denial is not advocated! Positive action is!

Keep it in mind!

t isn't the mountain ahead that wears you out—it's the grain of sand in your shoe.

Robert Service

A lways bear in mind that your own
resolution to succeed is more
important than any other one thing.

Abraham Lincoln

Your Success Instinct

Do you know about the "success instinct?" A squirrel does not have to be taught how to gather nuts. Nor does it need to learn that it should store them for the winter. A squirrel born in the spring has never even experienced a winter. Yet in the fall of the year you can observe that squirrel busily storing nuts for the lean winter months. Birds do not take nest-building lessons. They have no ability to read maps, yet they can return to exact locations year after year. These instincts assist the animal to successfully cope with its environment. This is the "success instinct."

You have a success instinct as well. Animals' goals are preset; yours are completely up to your creative imagination. An animal's success is limited to its built-in goal-images that we call instincts; your success is unlimited.

You are not a machine, however, you do have a "servo-mechanism."

Maxwell Maltz wrote that:

" . . . your physical brain and nervous system make up a servo-mechanism which you use, and which operates very much like an electronic computer, and a mechanical goal-seeking device. Your brain and nervous system constitute a goal-striving mechanism which operates automatically to achieve a certain goal, very much as a self-aiming torpedo or missile seeks out its target and steers its way to it. Your built-in servo-mechanism functions both as a 'guidance

system' to automatically steer you in the right direction to achieve certain goals, or make correct responses to environment, and also as an 'electronic brain' which can function automatically to solve problems, give you needed answers, and provide new ideas or 'inspirations'."

There are two general types of this mechanism. One functions when the target, goal or answer is known and your objective is to reach or accomplish it, and the other functions when the target, goal or answer is not known and the objective is to discover or locate it. Your brain and your nervous system operate in both ways.

When you know your target, you also know when you are on course, and when you are off track. You accomplish your goals by going forward, making errors, continually correcting them and moving forward once again. Your built-in goal-striving mechanism works for you. Once the pattern is established, it will work for you automatically.

Remember the story of *The Little Engine that Could*: "I think I can, I think I can." It had a servo-mechanism rooted in positive affirmation. It focused on the goal and engaged fully in accomplishing it without doubt or question. It could have chosen to say, "I don't think I can, I don't think I can" and come to a complete stop. In both cases, the mechanism was trained and it performed. Reach your goals. Train your servo-mechanism.

Keep it in mind!

We first must think "I can,"
then behave appropriately
along that line of thought.

Marsha Sinetar

Without passion man is a mere latent force and possibility, like the flint which awaits the shock of the iron before it can give forth its spark.

Henri-Frédéric Amiel

Your Passions

Eric S. Raymond said, "You cannot motivate the best people with money. Money is just a way to keep score. The best people in any field are motivated by passion."

What motivates you? What makes you delighted to open your eyes in the morning because you are looking so forward to doing it? What stirs your heart and your imagination? What keeps you going?

Some folks are clear about their passions. They have a strong sense of purpose. They know what lights their fire! In fact, they simply cannot *not* do it. George Balanchine, the great choreographer, said that he was not interested in dancers who wanted to dance, but in dancers who HAD to dance. That's the difference passion makes, isn't it?

What do you HAVE to do? There IS something, and once you find it you will soar.

The most fortunate people find their passion and make it their life. It may be their career. It may be raising a healthy, happy, functional family. It may be climbing mountains or protecting the environment. Whatever it is, it fills them with inspiration, ideas, imagination and fire. They have boundless energy for it. It may take some uncovering to find your deepest passions and it is time very well spent.

Explore the ideas, insights, experiences and visions that fill your heart with passion. What captures your mind, your heart and soul?

Take all the time you need to go deeper and deeper into your self. It is waiting for you to discover. If you already know what it is, explore the ways you can expand, broaden and deepen your commitment to it.

Keep it in mind!

Ability is what you're capable of doing. Motivation determines what you do. Attitude determines how well you do it.

Lou Holtz

I have to live for the day, and not worry about or try to know what tomorrow brings . . . if I've learned one thing from all that's happened to me, it's that if you would know what tomorrow brings, you may not want to live it.

Monica Seles

Why Worry?

James Lowell gave us some paradoxical advice:

*"Let us be of good cheer, remembering that the
misfortunes hardest to bear are those which never happen."*

This quote is an interesting twist on a useless activity that
many people feel is required of them in order to be responsible.
That activity is called *worrying!*

I wonder how many teenagers have been brought home safely
late at night by a mother staying up and worrying where they are
and what they are doing. I wonder how many people have turned
around adversity in their lives by wringing their hands, not eating
and having insomnia. There is an ethic ingrained in many of us
that worrying is a virtue . . . it somehow shows we care deeply
about something.

If we could understand another principle, worry would be
a thing of the past. It's a simple one: each person has energy to
use, you use it in the way you choose. So, why choose to use it
worrying? When something looms, or occurs, that causes you
concern, make a plan to do something about it. Take action!
Figure out what will change the situation, or
create a positive outcome, and use your energy
for that. Take the first, even the smallest, step
you can towards solution, rather than waste
that energy worrying. Be pro-active, too. Think
ahead. Take care of things in a timely manner so
that you prevent yourself from creating situations
that cause tension.

For today, if you find yourself worrying, take a deep breath in through your nose, release the breath slowly through your mouth, and relax.

Then ask yourself, what is the first thing I know to do about this to create a positive outcome? And, do it! Take action!

Keep it in mind!

People do not live a hundred years, but they worry as if they would live a thousand.

Chinese proverb

Remember, people will judge you by your actions, not your intentions. You may have a heart of gold—but so does a hard-boiled egg.

Unknown

The Road Paved with Good Intentions

Rev. Jesse Jackson is quoted as saying, "If you can see it in your mind and feel it in your heart, it can be." What do you see in your mind and feel in your heart for yourself?

Watch out! The question asks what YOU want, not what the world tells you demonstrates success. For many folks, that is quite a shift. If the advertising world has it right, success is money, fame, "status" cars, luxury homes with so many rooms you can seldom sit in each of them once a week, designer clothes with other folks' names on them, THE latest of everything. Is that your idea of success? If it is, then you're on the right path. If not, it is well worth your time to figure out what you will have, do and be to achieve success on your own terms! With your personal definition of success, what will your life be like when you have achieved it?

Once you've determined that, begin to create a statement of intention for your life right now. That statement is a general one that will answer the question, "Why?" when asked your reasons for doing what you're doing at any given moment.

Here's an example:

Q: "Why are you spending so much time and energy on your food and exercise?"

A: "Because I want to take very good care of myself and bring clarity of thought to my work.

Intentions:

To take very good care of myself

To work smarter, not harder

To be healthy

An intention is a determination to act in a certain way, or a statement of what you are going to bring about in your life. It is a broader concept that specific goals and objectives. It is the overall design concept for your current life.

Do you have honorable intentions for yourself? There is no right answer, simply *your* answer. Your intention does not state the specifics as a goal does, nor does it contain an action plan to outline how you will achieve it. It is the big light in the distance. Once you know what it is and know you want it, then you can always look up and see it as you consciously move towards it. When you keep it in view, it will brighten your path. A little light helps keep the path in view.

It's not that proverbial road to a particular destination that is paved with good intentions! Intentions are the bedrock for the smooth asphalt that will come along later and allow you to continue building roads. You can only get hellacious results when intentions are all you have! If you have no plan, no map, and no light, it's all just a great idea! Start building!

Keep it in mind!

Plans are only good intentions unless they immediately degenerate into hard work.

Peter Drucker

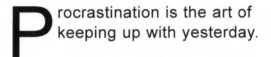

Procrastination is the art of keeping up with yesterday.

Don Marquis

Why Not Now?

"NOW" is the magic word of success. That road paved with good intentions is littered with words like tomorrow, next week, later, sometime or someday!

Let's consider an example you know well--saving money. Probably everyone would agree that saving money is a good idea. So, do you have an organized saving and investment program? It seems that many people have the *intention* to save consistently and few actually *act* on these intentions. There are unpleasant statistics to tell us that most folks will retire on very little!

It is always going to be true that it is easier to spend what's left over after saving than it is to save what's left over after spending! It is good advice, often repeated, that paying yourself 10% of your income FIRST is a very wise decision. Even if you are eating simply by the first month's end, you will have demonstrated the care you are willing to take for your overall well-being! You are very adaptable. You'll soon be adjusted to the new routine of saving and spending. Think of it as "spending" on your savings!

Ben Franklin told us: "Don't put off until tomorrow what you can do today." Thinking in terms of NOW gets things accomplished. Thinking in terms of "someday" or "sometime" often creates failure. Make "ACT NOW!" a habit!

Keep it in mind!

You can have anything you want if you want it desperately enough. You must want it with an inner exuberance that erupts through the skin and joins the energy that created the world.

Sheila Graham

Where Do You Get Your Energy?

The energy you bring to your daily life has a tremendous impact on the people you encounter no matter where you happen to be. The strength with which you act, look, move and carry yourself is a statement. The way others see you greatly affects the way they treat you. So what are you projecting?

A quick route to personal power is to develop the energy it takes to be successful in life. Do you know how? Do you know where to find the well-spring of physical well-being that will enable you to achieve the results you want in life, to turn indifference into attention, conflict into cooperation, rejection into acceptance, and dreams into reality? Tall order . . . and it can be done.

One quick and steady way to have more energy is to improve your breathing. It seems obvious that you could not expect more energy without breathing more oxygen. That would be like expecting the logs in your fireplace to burn without opening the flue. Food that's been converted mostly to fat gets "burned" with oxygen to release energy. Of course, you will have to do something to get that burning, won't you?

Begin by sitting quietly with your eyes closed and pay attention to your breathing. Breathe a little deeper than usual . . . just a little. Enjoy it. Not only will you take in more oxygen but you will relax as well. Not only will you feel fresher and better able to handle whatever comes your way, but you will have conserved energy for moments of tension. A great equation!

Your diet makes a difference to your energy level, too. Your diet is a daily choice. Eliminating excess dietary fat is a great beginning. It is not the quantity of food you consume, it's the quality.

Exercise is important. You've heard that . . . unless you've been living underground alone for the last fifty years! Exercise in ways that are appropriate for your age and condition and gently build up your stamina and fitness level. That will give you energy. If you will do a half hour of yoga most days, you will notice that you require less sleep and have sustained energy during the day. Not a bad trade-off, is it?

Increase your energy. Personal power is more than the psychological feeling that you are going to succeed. It requires a catalyst and that catalyst is the energy you bring to life. Without energy, it's very unlikely you will achieve your goals. Isn't that a compelling reason to take good care of yourself?

Keep it in mind!

To bring one's self to a frame of mind and to the proper energy to accomplish things that require plain hard work continuously is the one big battle that everyone has. When this battle is won for all time, then everything is easy.

Thomas A. Buckner

A man's work is his dilemma - his job is his bondage, but it also gives him a fair share of his identity, and keeps him from being a bystander in someone else's world.

Melvin Maddocks

Is Your Work Important?

Do you think your work is important? I often tell this story in my workshop on "Creating Teams That Work":

A fellow came upon a construction site with many laborers working. He approached one fellow and asked him what he was doing there. The fellow said, "I'm making this mud into bricks." He asked a second fellow what he was doing, and he said, "I'm sawing this lumber to the correct size and I'm making $7.00 an hour." After watching the work for a while, he determined the hardest working fellow and asked him the same question. His answer: "I'm building a beautiful cathedral."

It is all in your perspective, isn't it? What is your vision of your work?

It is probably safe to assume that the fellow who could focus on the building of the cathedral rather than the mud, lumber and hard labor would likely move up on the job. He might become the foreman, a contractor or, even, an architect. He was THINKING about what he was creating.

The same is true on a personal basis in your own life. You are what you see yourself as. Think you are weak, think you lack what it takes, think you'll lose, think you are undeserving, you are doomed to mediocrity. If you think instead, "I am important. I have what it takes to succeed. I am a first class performer. My work is important . . . " you are headed straight for success.

The key to creating what you want in life lies in thinking positively about yourself. The only real basis other people have for judging your abilities is your actions. Your actions are controlled by your thoughts.

You ARE what you THINK you are.

Keep it in mind!

I f you do not value yourself independently of your achievements, you will not value your achievements.

Gilliam Butler

Procrastination makes easy things hard, hard things harder.

Mason Cooley

Don't Just Wait!

Do you ever wait for things to be perfect before you act? Why is that? There is often a kind of passivity in waiting, isn't there? You can fool yourself into thinking that you will, in fact, do it . . . just not right now! You may often use the phrase, "when the time is right." You are the only person who really knows how you use these tactics. Only you know if you are a person of action, or a person of procrastination. Which are you?

Successful people take action. They know what they want. They plan. They study. They act. Passive folks postpone doing things until they can prove that they can't or shouldn't do them, or . . . until it's just too late! When you take action you are not only more likely to achieve your goals, you also gain self-confidence, inner security, and self-reliance.

The test of a successful person is not the ability to eliminate all problems before they arise, but to meet and work out difficulties when they *do* arise. You must be willing to make an intelligent compromise with perfection lest you wait forever before taking action. It's good advice to cross bridges as you come to them, isn't it?

There are two things to do that will help you avoid the costly mistake of waiting until conditions are perfect before you act. Be pro-active about future obstacles and difficulties. Every venture presents risks, problems or uncertainties. If you were driving from Chicago to Los Angeles, would you wait until you had absolute assurance that there would be no detours, no car problems, no bad weather, no

drunken drivers? If that were the case, you would never start. In planning that trip it makes sense to map your route, check your car, and do everything you can to eliminate risks, but you cannot eliminate them all, for sure! Be prepared to meet obstacles as they arrive. The test of a successful person is not the ability to eliminate all problems before you take action, but rather the ability to find solutions to difficulties when you encounter them. In business, marriage, or in any other activity, cross bridges when you come to them.

Make up your mind to do something with your ideas. Ideas are important. We must have ideas before we can create or improve anything. Ideas alone are not enough. Give your ideas value by acting on them. Someone once said that the saddest words of tongue or pen are these: *it might have been.*

Use action to cure fear and gain confidence. Action feeds and strengthens confidence; inaction, in all forms, feeds fear. To fight fear, act. Build confidence. Remove fear through planned action. You cannot start any younger!

Keep it in mind!

Y ou can be greater than
anything that can happen to
you.

Norman Vincent Peale

The world is divided into people who do things and people who get the credit. Try, if you can, to belong to the first class. There's far less competition.

Dwight Morrow

Get Going!

People who get things done in this world do not wait for the spirit to move them. They move the spirit!

A humorist once said that the most difficult problem in life was getting out of a warm bed into a cold room . . . and he had a point. The longer you lie there and think how unpleasant it will feel to hit that cold air, the more difficult it becomes. Even in such a simple activity as this one, taking action—throwing off the covers and putting your feet on the floor—defeats the fear. Sometimes you have to start yourself almost mechanically. You have to use your mind to overcome your reluctance. Use action to cure fear and gain self-confidence.

The same principles apply to using your mind as apply to many mechanical devices you use. You have central heating but you are the one who must select the temperature you want. Your car shifts gears only after you have chosen which gear to use. You must get your mind in gear to make it produce for you. You must be clear about what you want before you can make it happen.

This is why it is important to write your goals and resolutions down. Writing focuses your full attention on the thought. It is written on the page and imprinted in your subconscious mind. Reading your goals each week reinforces the thought and strengthens the focus of the mind. This is how dreams become realities.

Keep it in mind!

Knowing is not enough; We must apply. Willing is not enough; We must do.

Goethe

How Positive Is Your Outlook?

Henry J. Kaiser has said,

"When a tough, challenging job is to be done, I look for a person who possesses an enthusiasm and optimism for life, who makes a zestful confident attack on his daily problems, one who shows courage and imagination, who pins down his buoyant spirit with careful planning and hard work, but says, 'This may be tough, but it can be licked.'"

Is that your outlook?

Some people confuse positive thinking and denial. Positive thinking focuses on the desired outcome, while being aware of the current reality. Denial is a refusal to face what is so. Big difference! Denial, then, allows folks to postpone dealing with things indefinitely.

Positive thinking is a powerful tool once you realize how the mind works. The brain cannot tell the difference between an actual "real-time" event and the playing of the same event in the mind. That is why affirmation and visualization work! Focus on the outcomes you want. Do not entertain images of what you wish to avoid.

The human cortex is composed of some ten billion neurons, each with numerous axons which form synapses between the neurons. When you think, remember or imagine, these neurons discharge an electrical current which can be measured. The same is true when you learn something. Neurons form a new pattern in your brain tissue. This pattern is remembered. They are replayed, or reactivated, whenever you remember a past experience.

Recent brain research states that the brain contains over a trillion cells and that, by the end of an average life span, most people have only activated or partially activated 2.5% of them! Are you using your mind to its fullest? It takes fewer brain cells to understand a positive statement than a negative one. Are you using that information to affirm yourself and your desired outcomes?

Keep it in mind!

When you arise in the morning, give thanks for the morning light, for your life and strength. Give thanks for your food, and the joy of living. If you see no reason for giving thanks, the fault lies with yourself.

Tecumseh, Shawnee Chief

P oor is the man who does not know his own intrinsic worth and tends to measure everything by relative value. A man of financial wealth who values himself by his financial net worth is poorer than a poor man who values himself by his intrinsic self worth.

Sidney Madwed

You Deserve It

How does the care you take of your physical and emotional well-being reflect your self-esteem? Likely the two are very closely related when you dig right down to the bare truth. You know that appearances are deceiving. It is easy to look as though you care for yourself. Only you know if you really do.

A year or so ago, I was given some lovely little indoor garden kits and I was planting them. It occurred to me that I really could have given those to someone else to enjoy. In fact, I recognized an old part of me that felt that I "should" have done just that! This is where the self-esteem self-talk fortunately leapt in! It sounded like this:

"Yes, you could do that–keep them for a long time and give them away. They would make a nice gift."

"True, but, I would enjoy planting them and watching them grow. I deserve to enjoy this and that's why my friend gave me this wonderful gift. "

"What part of me is thinking that I 'shouldn't' have this pleasure?"

"Oh, the scarcity and the 'afraid I'm being selfish' part.

"Oh, wow, that's coming from a very old, childhood place, isn't it?"

"Yes, OK, enough of that. I'm going to plant them and enjoy them. Each time I look at them I will remember the delightful person who gave them to me. I deserve to enjoy these and take pleasure in the process. I am grateful to my friend for these, as well as for the love she expressed in giving them to me."

This old stuff comes up now and again, doesn't it? Does this in any way sound familiar to you? Do you feel deserving of love, attention and gifts? Do you have an internal conversation that allows you to accept joy, pleasure, gratitude, love? I hope so. Even though there may be some 'mental gymnastics' involved, think through the process and treat yourself well.

When the time to exercise comes along, remind yourself that you deserve to be healthy, strong and energetic. You can spend time on you. When dessert becomes breakfast, remind yourself of the same thing!

You deserve to create a life filled with pleasure, abundance, compassion and care. Give these to yourself!

Keep it in mind!

Self-esteem is as important to our well-being as legs are to a table. It is essential for physical and mental health and for happiness.

Louise Hart

We don't know who we are until
we see what we can do.

Martha Grimes

Just See It!

How is your creative imagination? Can you see things in your mind's eye and make them "real" to your brain, nervous system and senses? This is an excellent facility to develop further and use in your goal achievement process.

Here's an important fact: Your nervous system cannot tell the difference between a real and an imagined event. That's why your body goes through the same distress each time you retell the story of a frightening or sad event. It may not be at the same level of distress but the signals to the body will be the same. Of course, this is also true of the positive messages and stories you tell yourself and others.

How can you use this information to your highest good? You can use the operation of this unconscious creative mechanism by calling up, capturing and evoking the feeling of success. Envision your goals achieved and how you will feel when that is accomplished. See yourself enjoying the benefits. Feel the exhilaration and relief in your body. Use the natural workings of your mind to accomplish your goals.

Take the time to fully see, hear, feel, touch, taste and smell the things you want in life. Just sit with your eyes closed and imagine all the "sense-ations" that will accompany your success. Get fully into it. It's simple and it works!

Keep it in mind!

Man's mind, once stretched by a new idea, never regains its original dimensions.

Oliver Wendell Holmes

Use Your Mind Well

Your mind is an amazing mechanism. Your mind can carry you forward to outstanding success. Of course, it can also do just the reverse!

You know that your body is as good as the nutrition it receives. Do you know that the mind is also dependent on what it is fed? Your "mind food" is your environment–all the things which influence your conscious and subconscious thought. The kind of "mind food" you consume determines your habits, attitudes, and personality. The mind reflects what its environment feeds it in the same way the body reflects the nutrition you give it. The "size" of your thinking–your goals, attitudes, self-talk, values– is formed by your environment, your psychological environment. Your ability to change depends on what you feed yourself.

Thinking that major accomplishments are beyond your reach is a primary roadblock on the road to high level success. As Henry Ford said, "Think your can or think you can't–either way, you'll be right!"

You may have had many suppressive forces at work during your childhood or young adult life. Perhaps you were told that your ideas were impractical, stupid, naive or foolish. You may have bought the limiting belief that you need a lot of money to "get places" in this world. You may have been taught that success had a whole lot to do with something called "luck". I prefer Seneca's definition of luck as being "when preparation meets opportunity"!

Were you bombarded with "you-can't-get-ahead-so-don't-bother-to-try" propaganda? Many folks were. People have responded to this message in one of three ways. First, they bought it completely. You can easily spot them because they go to great lengths to rationalize their status and explain how "happy" or "content" they really are. The second group enters adult life with considerable hope for success. They prepare, plan and work hard. After a decade or so, they look around and rationalize, "I'm earning more than the average and I live better than the average, so why not just coast?" The journey to whatever they consider to be the top has begun to look daunting and they may have developed a set of fears: fear of failure, fear of social disapproval, fear of insecurity, fear of losing what they already have. Deep down, they know they have surrendered. There are many talented, intelligent people who elect to crawl through life because they are afraid to stand up and run.

The third group are those who marched on. They reach their own personal "top" and often exceed it. To be part of this group, you need to examine any suppressive influences in your environment and replace them with supportive, encouraging, uplifting ideas, people, events and relationships. Keep your "eyes on the prize" and remove obstacles systematically. Be a self-encourager.

Which group is yours? It's your choice.

Keep it in mind!

Many an opportunity is lost because [one] is out looking for four-leaf clovers.

Unknown

The thought manifests as the word;
The word manifests as the deed;
The deed develops into habit;
And habit hardens into character. So
watch the thought and its ways with
care, And let it spring from love Born
out of concern for all beings.

The Buddha

Show Your Self Respect

Thinking that you deserve respect is an important example of the power of your thought. The more self-respect you accord yourself, the more respect you will receive in your day-to-day interactions with others. How you think determines how you act. How you act, in turn, determines how others react to you.

Self-respect shows through in everything you do. Do you honor yourself by keeping your commitments to yourself? That is an important component. Do you respect your body by giving it healthy, nourishing food and by moving it systematically to improve it? Do you speak well of yourself–not arrogantly, but in positive terms? That even includes the way you talk to yourself in your mind!

Do you present yourself in a respectful way? Do you dress appropriately and take care with your appearance? This is a very powerful demonstration of self-respect. The way you look says powerful things about you. Yes, you've heard that it is unwise to judge a book by its cover, however, there is also wisdom in knowing that you never get a second chance to make a first impression! Taking good care of yourself is basic to self-respect.

Your appearance speaks for you. It helps determine what others think of you. In theory, it's comforting to hear that folks should look at your mind, your behavior, your values–and those speak essential volumes as well–however, your appearance is often the first basis for evaluation.

When people first become acquainted on the internet, there is opportunity to learn about each other in ways deemed much more important than the visual. It's true, though, that stories abound about the disappointment and "lack of chemistry" that follows meeting in person. Why? Because the person just did not look the way they sounded. Appearance counts. Think of the job interview situation as well for further evidence.

An interesting story:

> *In a supermarket one day, David Schwartz noticed one table of seedless grapes marked at $1.29 a pound. On another table were what appeared to be identical grapes, packaged in attractive plastic wrap at two pounds for $3.00. He asked the produce manager what the difference was between the two grapes. He was told that the difference is the wrapping. They sold twice as many of the wrapped grapes because they looked better that way.*

So the conclusion might be that the better the packaging, the better the sale! Does that have implication for the care and attention you give you yourself?

Keep it in mind!

They cannot take away our self-respect if we do not give it to them.

Gandhi

'd gone through life believing in the strength and competence of others; never in my own. Now dazzled, I discovered that my capacities were real. It was like finding a fortune in the lining of an old coat.

Joan Mills

Thinking Makes It So

Your thoughts create your day. You perceive something with your senses. You react to your perception by forming a thought about it. You respond to the thought with your feelings. You may or may not take action. The action or inaction has consequences. You perceive the consequences, and, guess what . . . you form a thought! That is the cycle.

You may have heard the phrase, "You are what you think." Further to that, your thinking projects outwardly so that everyone is affected by it. Have you ever noticed that some people get that "What do you want?" treatment while others get a sincere and respectful, "Yes, may I help you?" Some people project confidence, others do not. An employee will carry out the instructions of one superior perfectly yet only grudgingly pay attention to the requests of another. This can all be the result of thought.

Thinking DOES make it so. The fellow who thinks he is inferior, regardless of what his real qualifications may be, projects inferiority. Thinking regulates actions. If a woman feels inferior, she acts that way, and no veneer, cover-up or bluff will hide this basic feeling for long. The person who feels s/he isn't important, is likely to be treated that way.

How you think determines how you act.
How you act determines how others react to you.
What are you thinking?

Keep it in mind!

There is no such thing as *can't* only *won't*. If you're qualified, all it takes is a burning desire to accomplish, to make a change. Go forward, go backward. Whatever it takes! But you can't blame other people or society in general. It all comes from your mind. When we do the impossible we realize we are special people.

Jan Ashford

That Winning Feeling

Do you have that "winning" feeling? Do you know how to get it? Do you know how to keep it? I hope so!

When you supply the goal and think in terms of the end result, your automatic creative mechanism will supply the means to bring it about. You must think of the end result in terms of a present possibility. The possibility of the goal must be seen so clearly that it becomes "real" to your brain and nervous system. It must become so real that the same feelings are evoked within you that would be present if the goal were already achieved. This is the power of the mind.

It is not magical or mystical. We do it all the time anyway. When you worry, you are focused on an outcome with possible unfavorable results, right? Then you go through the anxiety, inadequacy or embarrassment in advance as though the worst had already happened. You picture the failure and experience the pain. If you are an expert worrier, you repeat this process over and over. Why not use this capacity of the mind to create the positive outcomes you want?

Your mind automatically acts and reacts to the environment, circumstance or situation. You are the one who decides what information to feed your mind. You decide what you believe to be true and the outcomes you want. So, focus on the positive!

Keep it in mind!

I f a man does not keep pace with his companions, perhaps it is because he hears a different drummer. Let him step to the music which he hears, however measured or far away.

Henry David Thoreau

Be Different!

To what extent are YOU making choices about your activities, your values and your attitudes rather than being affected, and thus controlled, by what others may think? It is difficult to be a real power performer if you think it is important to behave like everyone else.

Do you back down because some folks do not agree with what you want to do? Being confident in your ideas and your ability to think them through is the starting place for innovation. Who do you ask when you have a new and, maybe, different idea? Do you go to someone who is likely to agree with you, or someone who is likely to tell you that you are mistaken? Do you want to be supported . . . or stopped? Many people count on others to keep them from turning in new directions or taking new risks. What is your pattern?

The extent to which other people affect you is important to examine. Some people are very dependent on those around them and are greatly influence by the moods, attitudes and opinions of others. Others keep their own counsel and are empathetic to others while remaining true to themselves. This is preferable, isn't it?

Keep friends around you who will ask you good questions and show interest in your ideas rather than giving you their judgments and raining on your parade. Sure, you may want their opinions to consider. That's helpful to your thinking. It's the folks who believe that their opinions are "facts" that are the difficulty.

Surround yourself with people who are living fully. Pull each other in the directions of your dreams. The extent to which you feel that you control your future is the measure of what you will get out of life. To some folks, life is like the weather—it just happens to them, and they think they have no control.

Really, though, life is a majestic journey, an exciting adventure, that you orchestrate and direct by the hundreds of choices you make every day.

Keep it in mind!

Some people weave burlap into the fabric of our lives, and some weave gold thread. Both contribute to make the whole picture beautiful and unique.

Anonymous

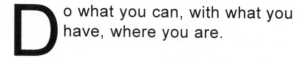

Do what you can, with what you have, where you are.

Theodore Roosevelt

Work With What You Have

Have you ever taken an acting class and been challenged to imagine as many uses as possible for some simple household object? It is a wonderful exercise in creativity. Try it. Go to the kitchen. Find a tool you use every day and imagine all possible uses for it. It is creative to find new ways of doing things using the resources we have at hand. The same is true for skills. Relationship or communication skills that work at work can be very effective at home.

A short while ago, I was having a conversation with a good friend. She was telling me that she was about to commit to a network marketing company and that she was sure that she had found the perfect career. It was terrific to hear the certainty and excitement in her voice. She went on, however, to tell me that now, before even signing the paper to begin, she needed a new apartment with a separate room for an office, a fax machine, a new printer and other office fixtures. Why? Because, to her, this was what it would take to be successful. I suggested that small steps might be more empowering than large debt . . . perhaps she could use the things she has until spending is warranted. Have you ever had the experience of thinking that you cannot begin a project until you have everything that you could possibly need before you start?

What could you do right now with the things you have at hand? What changes could you make in your life right now just by deciding to do so? We do not have to wait until we lose twenty pounds, clean out our basements and garages, and take back our library books, to move ourselves forward, although those things make admirable and important beginnings, too. You can do things simultaneously, can't you? Follow Ernest Hemingway's advice:

> *"Now is no time to think of what you do not have. Think of what you can do with what there is."*

For today, if you find yourself saying "I would like to do that if only I had _____ or if only I was _____", or anything close to that, change your focus. Ask yourself, "What steps could I take right now towards what I want to bring into my life, using my present skills, talents, desires and resources?" It's a great place to begin.

Keep it in mind!

This is our purpose: to make as meaningful as possible this life that has been bestowed upon us; to live in such a way that we may be proud of ourselves; to act in such a way that some part of us lives on.

Oswald Spengler

About the Author . . .

Dr. Rhoberta Shaler solves 'people problems' and makes it easier to talk about difficult things.

Rhoberta Shaler, PhD, speaks, coaches & conducts seminars for entrepreneurs & professionals who want the motivation, strategies and inspiration to achieve, to lead and to live richly. She has spent over 30 years teaching, encouraging and inspiring thousands of people to look at their personal and corporate lives from a new perspective. Rhoberta challenges them to create integrity between their plans and their daily practices, their beliefs and their behaviors. Her commitment to finding passion in life and pursuing it is contagious.

An expert facilitator, Dr. Shaler helps executives & entrepreneurs and their employees develop the effective communication skills needed to create powerful conversations that reduce conflict, build trust, and streamline negotiation.

Clients say that Rhoberta Shaler, PhD, is "a gentle, effective and enthusiastic teacher" who is "down-to-earth while knowledgeable, practical, energetic . . . and humorous." An acclaimed and popular keynote speaker, her light-hearted approach and value-packed content help audiences quickly grasp valuable skills & strategies. After more than twenty-five years in the business, Dr. Shaler continues to develop new programs to meet the needs of her clients and to meet the challenges she sees in the marketplace.

The Optimize! Institute founded by Dr. Shaler offers accessible executive & employee education to enhance communication and productivity, improve workplace relationships, manage conflict and build collaborative teams. With Dr. Shaler's guidance, performance & profit improve in a more peaceful, dynamic culture.

Dr. Shaler is one of only eight Premier Coaches across North America for eWomenNetwork and a founding member of the International Council of Online Professionals. Her PhD is in educational psychology, and her intensive training in all aspects of conflict management—negotiation, mediation, anger—was completed at the prestigious Justice Institute of British Columbia. She is the author of more than a dozen books & audio programs, as well as many manuals to improve specific 'people skills'. Her books have been translated and published in Mexico, Latin America, China, Indonesia and India. Her numerous articles are published in more than 17,000 web pages and 1000's of ezines around the world.

Dr. Shaler lives in Escondido, CA and has 3 adult children and 3 grandchildren. In her "me time," she swims, practices yoga, shops for books, and enjoys the company of friends.

Visit her online at www.OptimizeInstitute.com

Products available for you at Optimize! Institute:

Keynotes, books, audio programs, teleseminars, and coaching.
www.OptimizeInstitute.com

KEYNOTES, Seminars and Corporate Training

Dr. Shaler offers you the insights and strategies to name, claim, tame and lead away the rhinos that are getting in your way. Your people skills—communication, conflict & anger management, negotiation, personal responsibility & accountability—are essentials for dealing effectively with the rhinos in our lives . . . and winning!

Walk with Dr. Shaler through the cages and savannahs of life and get tools and skills to wrestle the rhinos that block your progress on the path to the goals, relationships, success and peace you most want. Available for corporations and associations.

Book a keynote today and start winning! Topics, bio, client list & testimonials at www.OptimizeInstitute.com/keynotes

Corporate & Community Seminars

For executives, entrepreneurs and employees, Dr. Shaler offers a complete range of 'people skills' seminars on communication, conflict and anger management, and negotiation. The skills, insights and strategies offered in these seminars will increase peace, productivity and profits for you and your organization.

From conference breakouts to multi-day intensives, Dr. Shaler delivers practical, content-rich, in-depth training to make it easier to talk about difficult things. Bring her seminars to your office or community and provide your people with the high-level skills they need to solve 'people problems' and learn to 'play nicely together in the company sandbox' (or any sandbox!) Seminars make a great value-added benefit for your clients, and really show that you're keeping their best interests at heart. Offer a 'Wrestling Rhinos' component to your Board Retreat and get both the humor and skills to motivate and make a difference in your organization.

Complete details are available 24/7 on the web at

www.OptimizeInstitute.com

Books, Audio Programs, Teleseminars

Wrestling Rhinos: Conquering Conflict in the Wilds of Work

Dr. Shaler's entertaining and easy to read style presents the "tough stuff" of managing conflict and communication in everyday contexts. She offers effective insights, skills and strategies to handle the kinds of conflict that we all face, at work and at home.

Optimize Your Day! Practical Wisdom for Optimal Living.

This beautiful book makes a terrific gift, coffee table book or even bathroom book! You'll find motivational quotes, thoughts and insights to change your day and your life. There is space for you to keep a journal as well.

Keep It In Mind: Memorable Messages for Staying on Track.

Just when you thought the detours seemed endless, Dr. Rhoberta Shaler draws you a simple map for the road to success. Avoid tempting parking places. Remove roadblocks. Straightforward, practical wisdom to enhance your life.

Audio Program: Conflict is NOT A 4-Letter Word.

Managing conflict can be a tricky and delicate job. These two insightful audio seminars will give you proven strategies for resolving conflicts successfully - and creating healthy relationships - at work and at home. On 2 CD's or 2 Cassettes

Audio Program: Creating Your Life

Includes three of Dr. Shaler's most popular talks: You Are the Mastermind of Your Masterpiece, Be Positively Selfish and Be A Real Goal Getter! This series of seminars WILL motivate you to keep on track. On 2 CD's or 2 Cassettes

Audio Program: Your Past Is NOT Your Potential

Get motivated to give yourself permission to MOVE ON! Allowing your past mistakes and regrets to hold you back from future success is a common stumbling block for millions of people. Learn how to let to, and "get on with it!"

Audio Program: How to Make An Entrance & Work A Room

Dr. Shaler's popular Power Networking seminar on CD. These tips, techniques, insights and proven strategies will give you the knowledge necessary to walk confidently into any new setting or relationship and know that you will be remembered for the RIGHT reasons.

Audio Program: Prosperity on Purpose™

Rhoberta Shaler, PhD presents Prosperity on Purpose™: Eight Essentials for Creating The Life You Most Want. This 8-CD set gives you the insights, inspiration and information you need to shift your results from acceptable to exceptional, in every area of life.

1-Hour Crash Courses (Teleseminars)

Teleseminars bring the skills, insights & strategies you need to grow your business and improve your life directly to you via the telephone. There are fourteen teleseminars available to you on a wide range of important and necessary topics to help you solve your 'people problems' at work and home.

Join the Optimize! Network

The Benefits of Membership

Get 24/7 access to a growing library of online articles, PLUS discussion forums, "Ask Rhoberta" direct access FAQs, useful downloads, polls, surveys, games, personal blogger and more . . . AND quarterly 90-minute Teleclinics just for members.

Go GOLD

You can upgrade to GOLD Membership! For a small extra cost you get 24/7 unlimited access to powerful audio interviews by Dr. Shaler with the top experts in a wide range of business & life improvement categories, AND some very valuable bonus packages. ***Register online today.***

Get the insights, strategies & motivation you need at www.OptimizeInstitute.com

Lightning Source UK Ltd.
Milton Keynes UK
UKHW040703230320
360761UK00001B/8